I am for the woods against the world,

But are the woods for me?

I have sought them sadly anew, fearing

My fate's mutability,

Or that which action and process make

Of former sympathy

THE SINGING FOREST

AN ANTHOLOGY INSPIRED BY
THE BLACK WOOD OF RANNOCH

The Singing Forest

SELECTED, EDITED
AND ILLUSTRATED BY
PAMELA STEEL

WITH PHOTOGRAPHS BY
SARAH MacDONALD

LOCH COTTAGE PRESS
MMIV

First published 2004 by Loch Cottage Press

www.thesingingforest.com

Copyright © Pamela Steel 2004
Photographs Copyright © Sarah MacDonald 2004
ISBN 0-9547769-0-9
Designed and typeset in Rialto by Dalrymple
Printed and Bound in Belgium by Snoeck-Ducaju & Zoon

Endpapers: First and last verses from 'The Kiss',
by Edmund Blunden

THE SINGING FOREST
is dedicated to the memory of
LIZ HUTCHESON

I had my first experience of a native pinewood, indeed of anywhere north of Edinburgh, in 1949. We camped on the south shore of Loch Rannoch with the edge of the Black Wood of Rannoch a pine cone's throw away. Was it then or was it later I learned that the wood was 'black' because the trees were dark pines in contrast to light oaks and that the pines preferred these colder, north-facing slopes while the oaks relished the sun?

From *A Pleasure in Scottish Trees* by Alistair Scott, 2002

It was known ... as the Singing Forest, for many of the old trees leant against their neighbours, and when there was any wind their entwined branches, rubbing together, gave forth a constant singing.

From *The Singing Forest* by H. Mortimer Batten, 1955

THE FOUR SEASONS

In the black season of deep winter a storm of waves is roused
along the expanse of the world.

Raw and cold is icy spring, cold will arise in the wind.

A good season is summer for long journeys; quiet is the tall fine wood,
which the whistle of the wind will not stir.

A good season for staying is autumn; there is work then for everyone
before the very short days.

From 'The Four Seasons', Irish, author unknown,
11th century, in A Celtic Miscellany, Translations from the Celtic Literatures,
by Kenneth Hurlstone Jackson, 1951

WINTER

In the black season of deep winter a storm of waves is roused
along the expanse of the world

Here is no colour, here but form and structure,
The bones of trees, the magpie bark of birches,
Apse of trees and tracery of network,
Fields of snow and tranquil trees in snow
Through veils of twilight, northern, still, and sad,
Waiting for night, and for the moon
Riding the sky and turning snow to beauty,
Pale in herself as winter's very genius,
Casting the shadows delicate of trees …

Private the woods, enjoying a secret beauty.

From *The Land* by V. Sackville-West, 1926

The first snow was sleet. It swirled heavily
Out of a cloud black enough to hold snow.
It was fine in the wind, but couldn't bear to touch
Anything solid. It died a pauper's death.

Now snow – it grins like a maniac in the moon.
It puts a glove on your face. It stops gaps.
It catches your eye and your breath. It settles down
Ponderously crushing trees with its airy ounces.

But today it was sleet, dissolving spiders on cheekbones,
Being melting spit on the grass, smudging the mind
That humped itself by the fire, turning away
From the ill wind, the sky filthily weeping.

'Sleet' by Norman MacCaig

I know no greater delight than the sheer delight of being alone
It makes me realise the delicious pleasure of the moon
that she has in travelling by herself: throughout time,
or the splendid growing of an ash-tree
alone, on a hill-side in the north, humming in the wind.

'Delight of Being Alone' by D.H. Lawrence

I, singularly moved

To love the lovely that are not beloved,

Of all the Seasons, most

Love Winter, and to trace

The sense of the Trophonian pallor on her face.

It is not death, but plenitude of peace;

And the dim cloud that does the world enfold

Hath less the characters of dark and cold

Than warmth and light asleep;

And correspondent breathing seems to keep

With the infant harvest, breathing soft below

Its eider coverlet of snow.

Nor is in field or garden anything

But,duly look'd into, contains serene

The substance of things hoped for, in the Spring,

And evidence of Summer not yet seen.

From 'Winter' by Coventry Patmore

The mouse is a sober citizen who knows that grass grows in order that mice may store it as underground haystacks, and that snow falls in order that mice may build subways from stack to stack: supply, demand, and transport all neatly organised. To the mouse, snow means freedom from want and fear.

From *A Sand County Almanac* by Aldo Leopold, 1949

Owl
is my favourite. Who flies
like a nothing through the night,
who-whoing. Is a feather
duster in leafy corners ring-a-rosying
boles of mice. Twice

you hear him call. Who
is he looking for? You hear
him hovering over the floor
of the wood. O would you be gold
rings in the driving skull

if you could? Hooded and
vulnerable by the winter suns
owl looks. Is the grain of bark
in the dark. Round beaks are at
work in the pelletry nest.

resting. Owl is an eye
in the barn. For a hole
in the trunk owl's blood
is to blame. Black talons in the
petrified fur! Cold walnut hands

on the case of the brain! In the reign
of the chicken owl comes like
a god. Is a goad in
the rain to the pink eyes,
dripping. For a meal in the day

flew, killed, on the moor. Six
mouths are the seed of his
arc in the season. Torn meat
from the sky. Owl lives
by the claws of his brain. On the branch

in the sever of the hands
twigs owl is a backward look.
flown wind in the skin. Fine
rain in the bones. Owl breaks
like the day. Am an owl, am an owl.

'Owl' by George MacBeth

All these small creatures are working – working in sun and rain, during the hours of darkness, even when winter's grip has damped down the fires of life to mere embers. Then this vital force is merely smouldering, awaiting the time to flare again into activity when spring awakens the insect world. Meanwhile, under the white blanket of snow, below the frost-hardened soil, in crevices in the bark of trees, and in sheltered caves, the parasites and the predators have found ways to tide themselves over the season of cold.

From *Silent Spring* by Rachel Carson, 1962

SPRING

Raw and cold is icy spring, cold will arise in the wind

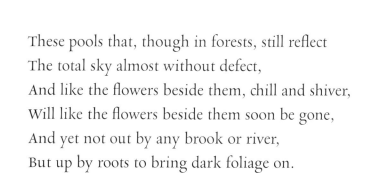

These pools that, though in forests, still reflect
The total sky almost without defect,
And like the flowers beside them, chill and shiver,
Will like the flowers beside them soon be gone,
And yet not out by any brook or river,
But up by roots to bring dark foliage on.

The trees that have it in their pent-up buds
To darken nature and be summer woods –
Let them think twice before they use their powers
To blot out and drink up and sweep away
These flowery waters and these watery flowers
From snow that melted only yesterday.

'Spring Pools' by Robert Frost

In this fresh evening each blade
and leaf looks as if it had been
dipped in icy liquid greenness.

From *Journal*, June 30, 1840,
by Henry David Thoreau

Then the moment of pure pleasure, when the sun strikes warm on some recess sheltered from the wind, and the willow warbler showers its silver notes on you from the arbour above your head.

From *A Year in Llyn*, in *Autobiographies* by R.S. Thomas, 1997

for now winter is past,
the rain is over and gone.
the flowers appear on the earth;
the time of singing has come,
and the voice of the turtledove
is heard in our land.

The Song of Solomon, 2.11-12

They went on calmly and, just before gaining the shelter of trees again, were vouchsafed a vision of glory. In front and high up on the right, there uprose from the sombre birches a golden-green fire. They had seen willow-catkins before many a time, but by some trick of the strong, sweeping sunlight, the exotic blaze was such that they debated what tree it could be. But not very ardently, for the burning bush was no more than something added to their own excitement. The secret spirit of the wood surprising but encouraging them with a voiceless shout! The catkins of the hazels, their flame blown from them, drooped like pencils of brown ash. A few withered nut-clusters were still on the boughs, reminding them not of a past autumn but of an autumn to come, for youth's memories have always this happy trick of living in the future.

From *Highland River* by Neil Gunn, 1937

The country habit has me by the heart.
He is bewitched forever who has seen,
Not with his eyes but with his vision, Spring
Flow down the woods and stipple leaves with sun,
As each man knows the life that fits him best,
The shape it makes in his soul, the tune, the tone,
And after ranging on a tentative flight
Stoops like the merlin to the constant lure.

From *The Land* by V. Sackville-West, 1926

Each grove, close and secret,
has its mantle of green,
the wood-sap is rising
from the roots at the bottom,
through arteries twisting
to swell out the growth;
thrush and cuckoo at evening
sing their litany above

From 'Song of Summer' by Alexander MacDonald
(Alasdair Mac Mhaighstir Alasdair)
Translated from the Gaelic by Derick Thomson

Listening to the dawn chorus it is easy to be filled with the joys of spring and think that the birds are, too. Nothing could be further from the truth. You are listening to dozens of contests between individuals of each species. They sing and, at the same time, listen to each other to find out exactly what is going on. It is listening that requires most bird songs to be short (chaffinch style) or long performances with frequent pauses (thrush-like). Each blackbird, robin, great tit and even chiffchaff will recognise their established neighbours – just as we know our friends when they speak.

From *In Song* by Chris Mead, 2001

Built like an oven with a little hole
Hard to discover – that snug entrance wins
Scarcely admitting e'en two fingers in
And lined with feathers warm as silken stole
And soft as seats of down for painless ease
And full of eggs scarce bigger e'en than peas
Here's one most delicate with spots as small
As dust – and of a faint and pinky red
– We'll let them be and safety guard them well
For fear's rude paths around are thickly spread
And they are left to many danger's ways

From 'The Pettichap's Nest' by John Clare

Even the sparrow finds a home,
and the swallow a nest for herself,
where she may lay her young.

Psalm 84.3

SUMMER

A good season is summer for long journeys: quiet is the tall fine wood,
which the whistle of the wind will not stir

And now I seem poised to enter that mysterious state of happiness Meaulnes had glimpsed. I have the whole morning to explore the wood ... I follow what once must have been the bed of a stream, hidden under the lower branches of a tree I can't name – maybe an alder.

In the silence I hear a bird and imagine it to be a nightingale – though how can it be when they only sing at night? – which repeats the same phrase over and over, a morning greeting coming down through the leaves ...

From *Le Grand Meaulnes* by Alain-Fournier, 1913, translated by Brian Morton

Oh the summer time is coming
And the trees are sweetly blooming
And the wild mountain thyme
Grows around the purple heather,
Will you go, lassie, go?

And we'll all go together,
To pull wild mountain thyme,
All around the blooming heather,
Will you go, lassie, go?

From 'Wild Mountain Thyme',
a Scots song

The smells I smell are of life, plant and animal. Even the good smell of earth, one of the best smells in the world, is a smell of life, because it is the activity of bacteria in it that sets up this smell.

Plants then, as they go through the business of living, emit odours. Some, like the honey scents of flowers, are an added allurement to the insects; and if, as with heather, the scent is poured out most recklessly in the heat of the sun, that is because it is then that the insects are out in strength. But in other cases – as the fir trees – the fragrance is the sap, is the very life itself. When the aromatic savour of the pine goes searching into the deepest recesses of my lungs, I know it is life that is entering. I draw life in through the delicate hairs of my nostrils. Pines, like heather, yield their fragrance to the sun's heat.

Of plants that carry their fragrance in their leaves, bog myrtle is the mountain exampler. This grey-green shrub fills the boggy hollows, neighboured by cotton-grass and sundew, bog asphodel and the spotted orchis, and the minute scarlet cups of the lichens. Its fragrance is cool and clean, and like the wild thyme it gives it most strongly when crushed.

From *The Living Mountain*,
by Nan Shepherd, 1977

They were safely in another good tree by the lochside. So brightly shone the sun, amongst the orange branches and on the blue water, it dazzled their eyes and made every cone glitter, so that they seemed to be plucking nuts of sunshine.

For about half an hour they sat there, no longer working. The scent of the tree seemed to strengthen with the darkness, until Calum fancied he was resting in the heart of an enormous flower. As he breathed in the fragrance, he stroked the branches, and to his gentle hands they were as soft as petals.

From *The Cone Gatherers* by Robin Jenkins, 1955

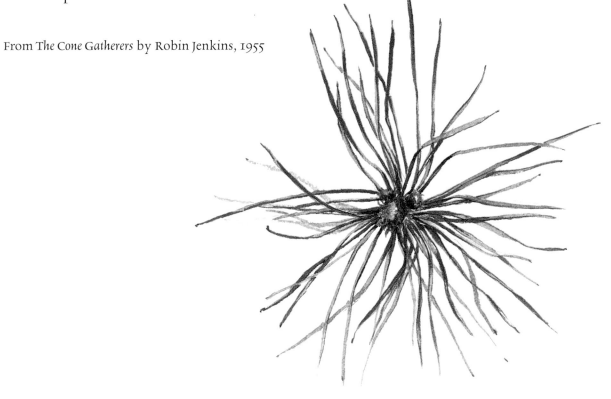

In the long trek to the Smuggler's Pool, he rested once or twice to absorb the silence and the feel of the atmosphere, as if an extra sense inside him would be receptive to the most exquisite disturbance. As indeed he knew it would be. His eyes leapt to the bird amongst its myriad leaves; his ears caught the song of the gnat; through his suspended breathing went the surge of the earth. And around him, at his feet, down the alleyways of the wood, were all the things, the dead and living things, so intimate to his blood. The leaves screened boulders in the river, gave him the half-glance of a pool.

From *Highland River* by Neil Gunn, 1937

I stood still and was a tree amid the wood,
Knowing the truth of things unseen before;
Of Daphne and the laurel bow
And that god-feasting couple old
That grew elm-oak amid the wold.
'Twas not until the gods had been
Kindly entreated, and been brought within
Unto the hearth of their heart's home
That they might do this wonder thing;
Nathless I have been a tree amid the wood
And many a new thing understood
That was rank folly to my head before.

'The Tree' by Ezra Pound

I sit with my back to a pine, I look at the setting sun, and I listen – to the murmur of the sea, to the sound of the wind in the pine branches. No doubt I listen in also to my conscience, that in me which knows, which thinks, and which sometimes would like to obliterate itself. But I go on, I go on listening, until I hear something. What? It's not hope I hear (I'd be ashamed of that); it's not a song, a chant, a hymn, a psalm; it's next to nothing. And it doesn't last. But it's all I need.

From *House of Tides* by Kenneth White, 2000

Straight trunks of the pine
      on the flexed hill-slope:
      green, heraldic helmets,
      green unpressed sea;
      strong, light, wind-headed,
      untoiling, unseeking,
      the giddy, great wood,
      russet, green, two plaitings.

Floor of bracken and birch
      in the high green room:
      the roof and the floor
      heavily coloured, serene:
      tiny cups of the primrose,
      yellow petal on green,
      and the straight pillars of the room,
      the noble restless pines …

The great wood in motion,
      fresh in its spirit;
      the high green wood
      in a many-coloured waulking;
      the wood and my senses
      in a white-footed rapture;
      the wood in blossom
      with a fleeting renewal.

The sunlit wood
      joyful and sportive,
      the many-winded wood,
      the glittering-jewel found by chance;
      the shady wood,
      peaceful and unflurried,
      the humming wood
      of songs and ditties.

From 'The Woods of Raasay' by Sorley MacLean
(Somhairle MacGill-Eain)

How long does it take to make the woods?
As long as it takes to make the world.
The woods is present as the world is, the presence
of all its past, and of all its time to come.
It is always finished, it is always being made, the act
of its making forever greater than the act of its destruction.
It is a part of eternity, for its end and beginning
belong to the end and beginning of all things,
the beginning lost in the end, the end in the beginning.

What is the way to the woods, how do you go there?
By climbing up through the six days' field,
kept in all the body's years, the body's
sorrow, weariness, and joy. By passing through
the narrow gate on the far side of that field
where the pasture grass of the body's life gives way
to the high, original standing of the trees.
By coming into the shadow, the shadow
of the grace of the strait way's ending,
the shadow of the mercy of light.

Why must the gate be narrow?
Because you cannot pass beyond it burdened.
To come into the woods you must leave behind
the six days' world, all of it, all of its plans and hopes.
You must come without weapon or tool, alone,
expecting nothing, remembering nothing,
into the ease of sight, the brotherhood of eye and leaf.

'How long does it take to make the woods?' by Wendell Berry

55

Yet as I crossed the River Tummel, travelled along the road that leads by the South bank of Loch Rannoch and entered the celebrated Black Wood of Rannoch, I forgot for a time the evil days through which Europe was passing in the strength and beauty of the old pines which form the Black Wood. One of the pines at the edge of the loch had been sawn off near the base, and out of curiosity I counted the rings of the great tree. Each ring of a tree denotes one year of its growth and this tree showed by its rings that it had lived 214 years.

There is a sense of security in the Black Wood. These great trees, centuries old, seem to tell of wisdom and peace. The wood is a relic of the old Caledonian Forest, and none of the trees have been planted by human hands. Some of them were well-grown when the Fiery Cross was sent round the district in 1745 and the men of the country rose to support Prince Charles Edward in his great adventure. In these natural-grown pine forests the trees do no grow so densely as to destroy the lesser vegetation, and the heather this day of late September, was purple beneath the old pines.

From *Highways and Byways in the Central Highlands* by Seton Gordon, 1948

1
I started off
by growing up
like everybody else.

2
Then I took

a bend to the south
an inclination east
a prolongation north
and a sharp turn west.

3
Now, approaching me
be prepared for grotesquerie

there are more than pines in my philosophy.

4
Yes I'm something more than a pine
I'm a cosmological sign.

5
I'm idiomatic
I'm idiosyncratic
I'm pre-socratic.

6
I'm maybe Chinese too

like Li Po, Tu Fu
and Mr Chuang-tzu.

7
I live quietly
but storms visit me

I do a metaphysical dance
at the heart of existence.

8
The branches of my brain
are alive to sun and rain

my forest mind
is in time with the wind

there is reason in my resin.

9
Behold the mad pine
stark on the sky-line.

'Interpretations of a Twisted Pine' by Kenneth White

As imperceptibly as Grief
The Summer lapsed away –
Too imperceptible at last
To seem like Perfidy –
A Quietness distilled
As Twilight long begun,
Or Nature spending with herself
Sequestered Afternoon –
The Dusk drew earlier in –
The Morning foreign shone –
A courteous, yet harrowing Grace,
As Guest, that would be gone –
And thus, without a Wing
Or service of a Keel
Our Summer made her light escape
Into the Beautiful

'As imperceptibly as Grief' by Emily Dickinson

If a swift comes down to the ground it finds it almost impossible to take off again. To make its rudimentary cup-like nest, it snatches feathers and grasses that drift in the air and cements them together with its sticky spittle. It drinks on the wing, dipping down to make a shallow dive through the surface of the pond. It feeds in mid-air entirely on flying insects. It sleeps in mid-air too, rising in the evening to heights of 6,500 feet and drifting in the wind with only occasional flickers of its outstretched wings. It even mates in mid-air. The male clings on to the female's back and united the two descend for a few seconds in a shallow glide. When a swift, young or adult, leaves its nest in early August, bound for Africa, it may not touch down again until it returns to its nest site nine months later.

From *The Life of Birds* by David Attenborough, 1998

A few days ago there was a warm southerly wind, dragging lower latitudes through the hills at a hell of a lick. When the rain came, it fled the already sodden ground and dived down brooks to fatten the river, threatening floods. When it finally stopped, a lone buzzard took to the topmost beech tree in the hanging woods. It perched there and called a strange plaintive, gull-like phrase; three or four sharp, sky-slicing notes, over and over.

The south is also exerting a powerful force over other birds. By late afternoon the sky is full of housemartins: a clan gathering, swooping through their communal dance. The martins urge stragglers to hurry up and join in. After a late start, rebuilding the nest and raising a pair of chicks, the martins are finally ready. One day the chicks are peeping out of their teapot home; the next they're flying with their hundred-strong clan above the woods and fields. The dance is to free the lodestones in their heads from the force which draws them to this place and holds them here all summer. Their minds spin to align with the mysterious longitude of their autumn migration road south. One day soon the sky will be empty.

Up in the morning fields an equally amazing collective journey has been written out. Over the foggy, freshly ploughed soil is what looks like frost. But it's gossamer: millions of long, inter-threaded strands, spun by spiders. Each length is an incredible voyage drawn across the earth, holding pearls of dew, waving and shimmering in the wind. It's a trap, devised and built by millions of spiders: a trap laid for the spirit of autumn.

'Autumn Journeys', from *Country Diary* by Paul Evans, 2000

AUTUMN

A good season for staying is autumn; there is work then for everyone
before the very short days

Pine crossbills are social animals whose survival partly depends on the coherence of the flock. In any month you are likely to meet with groups of varying size which are associated for different purposes ... the flock has helped crossbills to survive. Not only do the collective eyes of the group and their sharp-eyed sentries assist the members to avoid predators, but they also help to discover sources of food ... crossbills may possibly find new and more abundant crops from a long distance away by detecting subtle differences in the colour of the canopy. Groups of pioneers thus probably lead others to fresh feeding grounds and so enable them to survive in years of famine. Mixed flocks are difficult to watch, the crossbills moving like mice through branch and foliage, contacting one another by soft almost inaudible calls. All you now hear are cones tumbling from branch to branch, seed cases spiralling in the sun, and an intermittent loud leathery rustle of strong wings. The scarlet, orange, or brick-red cocks harmonise with cone, trunk and branch, and the green hens with the spines ...

From *Pine Crossbills* by Desmond Nethersole-Thompson, 1975

The same leaves over and over again!
They fall from giving shade above,
To make one texture of faded brown
And fit the earth like a leather glove.

Before the leaves can mount again
To fill the trees with another shade,
They must go down past things coming up.
They must go down into the dark decayed.

They *must* be pierced by flowers and put
Beneath the feet of dancing flowers.
However it is in some other world
I know that this is the way in ours.

'In Hardwood Groves' by Robert Frost

To a forester the most important fact about a spider is the kind of net it builds. The wheel-net spiders are most important, for the webs of some of them are so narrow-meshed that they can catch all flying insects. A large web (up to 16 inches in diameter) of the cross spider bears some 120,000 adhesive nodules on its strands. A single spider may destroy in her life of 18 months an average of 2,000 insects. A biologically sound forest has 50 to 150 spiders to the square metre.

From *Silent Spring* by Rachel Carson, 1962

When the trees grow bare on the high hills,
And through still glistening days
The wrinkled sun-memoried leaves fall down

From black tall branches
Through the gleaming air,
And wonder is lost,
Dissolving in space,
My heart grows light like the bare branches,
And thoughts which through long months
Have lain like lead upon my breast,
Heavy, slow-ripening thoughts,
Grow light and sere,
And fall at last, so empty and so beautiful.

From 'When the trees grow bare on the High Hills' by Edwin Muir

A great part of the pine-needles have just fallen. See the carpet
of pale-brown needles under this pine ... the ground is nearly
concealed by them. How beautifully they die, making cheer-
fully their annual contribution to the soil!

From *Journal*, October 16, 1857, by Henry David Thoreau

It is a century now since Darwin gave us the first glimpse of the origin of species. We know now what was unknown to all the preceding caravan of generations: that men are only fellow-voyagers with other creatures in the odyssey of evolution. This new knowledge should have given us, by this time, a sense of kinship with fellow-creatures; a wish to live and let live; a sense of wonder over the magnitude and duration of the biotic enterprise.

From A *Sand County Almanac* by Aldo Leopold, 1949

But alone in distant woods ... I come to myself, I once more feel myself grandly related, and that cold and solitude are friends of mine. I suppose that this value, in my case, is equivalent to what others get by church-going and prayer. I come to my solitary woodland walk as the homesick go home ... this stillness, solitude, wildness of nature is a kind of thoroughwort, or boneset, to my intellect. This is what I go out to seek. It is as if I always met in these places, some grand, serene, immortal, infinitely encouraging, though invisible, companion, and walked with him.

From *Journal*, January 7, 1857, by Henry David Thoreau

We thank thee, Lord, for the glory of the late days and the excellent face of thy sun. We thank thee for good news received. We thank thee for the pleasures we have enjoyed and for those we have been able to confer. And now, when the clouds gather and rain impends over the forest ... permit us not to be cast down; let us not lose the savour of past mercies and past pleasures; but, like the voice of a bird singing in the rain, let grateful memory survive in the hour of darkness.

From ' In Time of Rain' by Robert Louis Stevenson

My farewell to the forests! Oh marvellous
mountains they are, with green cress,
and spring water, a drink noble, splendid
and pleasing. The pastures that are
precious, and the wastes that are many.
gratefully I left them. Forever
my thousand blessings be with them!

From 'Last Leave of the Hills',
by Duncan Bàn MacIntyre
(Donnchadh Bàn Mac an t-saoir)
Translated from the Gaelic

Words interest me less and less each day,
like old coins
that have lost their shine.

The seagull's scrawlings on the sky's slate
mean more to me
than human hieroglyphs.

I can read more in trees, doodled
by the earth
on scraps of cloud

than I can in books. November winds
shake leaves
like last lessons

from branches. Woodsmoke is a poignant poem
of mortality:
elegy without words.

From 'Words' by Christopher Rush

On every hilltop
Now falls a hush
Across the treetops
The quiet of dusk
All flight is over
All song is ended
With nature's breath
Soon like these
You will find rest

'Wayfarer's Night Song II' by Goethe,
translated by Brian Morton

And can any amount of learning make us feel love,
or see beauty or hear the 'unheard melodies'?

From his Introduction to *The Upanishads*,
by Juan Mascaro, 1965

Late fall, season's broom
Sweeps every corner
Of an emptied house

Haiku 160 by Basho,
translated by Brian Morton

A WOODLAND REPUBLIC

The Black Wood of Rannoch is one of the largest of the thirty-five remnants of native pinewood remaining in Scotland today. In this wood there has been continuous tree cover for over 10,000 years. After the retreat of the last Ice Age Scots pines, which are adaptable and hardy and can live for up to four hundred years, spread over northern Europe and Russia. Cut off from the continent for 7,000 years or more, Scottish forests and trees, including the Rannoch pine, developed a character of their own. Over the last 5000 years, as humans began to claim more land for themselves, forests, woods and trees have steadily disappeared, and today little more than 17% of Scotland has any kind of afforestation (with well over 90% of this having been planted or re-planted in the last 50 years). The Black Wood has always been remote and relatively inaccessible, and this has done much to ensure its survival in previous centuries. The nearest remnant of native pinewood is a few miles to the south, at Meggernie in Glen Lyon.

The heart of the Black Wood covers a few square miles (290 hectares) of undulating, hummocky ground which slopes gently down to the southern shores of Loch Rannoch, in north-west Perthshire. The Dall burn runs down to the loch at the east end of the wood and the Camghouran burn to the west. Many smaller streams thread through the trees and connect with standing pools in the peaty hollows. In periods of dry weather these streams and pools can disappear completely. Otherwise this is a cool and moist area where the sound of water is a constant companion. Freedom from pollution ensures a high quality of air. Winters are long and can be harsh, spring comes late, and autumn arrives early. The light-filled summer days from May to August are precious to all, and filled with the intense activity of many millions of living things.

Throughout the wood young saplings cluster round their parent and grandparent trees, and though pines predominate, many silver and downy birch, some rowan, alder, willow and juniper, and a few aspen, are scattered everywhere. Areas of dense growth are interspersed with more open clearings where older trees have fallen. Light filters into these clearings allowing young seedlings to take hold in the soil and grow, and eventually take on their mature forms. Regeneration is natural. Seeds are spread by the wind, by birds and small animals. The long continuity of woodland cover and varied habitats, including the many stages of growth and decay of the trees, make the Black Wood a treasure-house of ecological diversity. A few small areas of the wood have been fenced off for research purposes, and are regularly monitored by scientists.

Tall heather, and blaeberry (or bilberry) and cowberry bushes form a dense ground cover on the forest floor and these, together with mosses and other common and rare woodland plants, and many different types of lichen (at least 150 types) and fungi, form a woodland habitat that can support a vast amount of animal life. Plants in the wood include primrose, wood anemone, wood sorrel and chickweed wintergreen, with rarer glimpses of lesser twayblade and coral root orchid.

Some red and roe deer inhabit the wood, but their numbers have to be carefully controlled as they browse the seedlings and young trees. Their only natural predators, the wolf and lynx have long been extinct in Scotland. Red squirrel, pine martin, fox, wild cat, voles, mice, moles, lizards, frogs, toads, bats and adders share this habitat with many different species of birds. The resident population, which includes buzzard, sparrow hawk, kestrel, capercaillie, black grouse, jay, long-eared and tawny owl, tree-creeper, four kinds of tit, siskin, redstart, goldcrest, and Scottish crossbill are joined by large numbers of winter and summer visitors. Redwing and fieldfare pass through the woods in the autumn and strip rowan trees of their berries before they head south for warmer climates. In spring warblers, swifts, swallows (and fish-eating osprey) fly from Africa to breed and rear their young in the area. The long days and quality and quantity of good things with which to feed their young make that journey worthwhile.

It is for this 'food', its invertebrate fauna, that the Black Wood is of outstanding importance. Beetles, flies, bugs, spiders, wood ants, and many other tiny creatures, some still without a name, some too small to see with the naked eye, make their homes in the forest. Moths, including the Rannoch Sprawler, dragonflies and damselflies are attracted to the sunny clearings, and the wood

ants' distinctive hills are scattered throughout the forest. Little is known about a great number of insects, and ongoing research is conducted primarily by academic institutions and skilled volunteer groups.

For many centuries the Black Wood has been used by humans for their own needs. Since the most ancient of times it has been a refuge, from the weather, from the fear of the Romans or the Norse, or from raids on the area by neighbouring clans intent on stealing cattle, or retrieving those stolen from them. Fires were used, to create grazing space, to drive out wolves, and to try to smoke out cattle thieves. Juniper was a useful wood to burn if anyone wished to escape detection in the woods as it makes the most invisible smoke. From the second half of the 17th century onwards felling periodically became more intensive as the demand for housing grew. Forest management again increased when the Dall estate became forfeited to the Crown after 1745.

In the 19th century an experiment was made to float logs out of the wood in a series of canals, the remains of which can still be seen. Times of national conflict always increased the demand for timber, with heavy felling taking place in the Napoleonic Wars. Timber operations again increased in the 1914–1918 war, and the whole wood was scheduled to be cut down in 1919. Again, in the 2nd World War, many of the best trees were felled by the Canadian Forestry Corps. By 1945 the wood was understocked and, because it had also been used for so many years as a sporting estate, it was overrun with deer. There were almost no young trees.

The Forestry Commission purchased the Black Wood in 1947. Immediately the core part of the wood was declared a conservation area and a programme to control the number of deer was introduced. Successive initiatives since then, in particular the vision of Gunnar Godwin in whose charge the wood was for many years, ensured its future as a protected Forest Reserve in 1975. A plaque in the heart of the wood honours his name.

Priorities for the Commission today are to 'maintain and enhance the historic, landscape and scientific interest of the Black Wood as a semi-natural Caledonian pinewood', to preserve the purity of the Rannoch strain of Scots pine, and to maintain the core area of the wood which will be allowed to grow naturally. The Commission is also committed to securing the regrowth of young trees in the area surrounding the heart of the wood, and in the Black Wood as a whole to removing other conifers that are not native to the wood, replacing them with Rannoch pine. Their long-term objective over the next 100 years is to have a semi-natural pinewood eco-system flourishing across the whole of this Caledonian Forest Reserve.

Half a century of protection, care, and minimum intervention in the core, has ensured a renaissance in the Black Wood. Though regeneration is slow, the identity and integrity of the wood are safe for the foreseeable future. Equally importantly, attitudes have changed to the secondary benefits that forests bring. Wildlife, recreation, and the recognition that trees and woods give pleasure and enhance health are now seen as important considerations. Though only one notice board at Dall proclaims the Black Wood and although wildlife conservation is of prime importance, and this woodland habitat is so delicate and vulnerable, people are welcome to enter the wood and wander the network of paths.

Pamela Steel, 2004

SOURCES

1999 Report of the Native Pinewood Managers', I. Ross, Scottish Forestry, Vol53, No.4. 1999

Black Wood of Rannoch Management Plan, 1995–2005, Forestry Commission and Scottish Natural Heritage

The Native Pinewoods of Scotland, Steven and Carlisle, 1959

ACKNOWLEDGEMENTS

My thanks are due to so many friends who have cheered *The Singing Forest* on its way over the last four years, but especially to Elspeth Davey, Elspeth Strachan and Jim Mein, to Jan Fairley for her helpful comments on drafts of the anthology, and to Charles Vyvyan for his early encouragement, and for introducing me to 'The Four Seasons'. Hamish Murray and Rob Coope of the Forestry Commission at Dunkeld have supported the idea from its inception, and read and commented on a draft of *A Woodland Republic*. Lastly, my love and thanks to Keith, Jamie, Charlie and Harry – and to Tigger and Tangle, the best of companions in the Black Wood. *Pammie Steel*

Thanks to my darling husband, Brian Morton, for advice, encouragement and infinite patience. Also to Steve Kelly and master craftsman Joe Robinson at the Techniques Group for printing the images. *Sarah MacDonald*

ILLUSTRATIONS

Details of the less easily identified illustrations are given here. In brackets beside some of the plant names are their Gaelic names, with English translations: Page 1 Wood Anenome (*Flùr na Gaoithe* 'Wind Flower'); page 4 Loch Cottage; page 5 Tormentil (*Cairt-làir* 'Ground Bark'); page 22 Long-eared Owl's feather; page 28 Chickweed Wintergreen (*Reul na Coille* 'Star of the Wood'); page 30 Primrose; page 38 Mistle Thrush feathers, wing and shoulder; page 40 Meadow Pipit's egg and Mallard feathers, wing and shoulder; page 41 Wren's nest; page 46 Wild Thyme (*Lus an Rìgh* 'The King's Plant'); page 47 Heath Spotted Orchid; page 54 Bog Asphodel; page 55 Heath Milkwort (*Siabann nam Ban-sìdh* 'Fairy Women's Soap'); page 60 Harestail Cotton Grass (*Sìoda Monaidh* 'Mountain Silk'); page 68 Chanterelle; page 78 Cowberry; page 79 Bog Bilberry and Blaeberry; page 86 Green-veined White butterfly, beetle, Rowan berries, Coal Tit's feather; page 94 Moss, *hylocomium splendens*.

COPYRIGHT ACKNOWLEDGMENTS

This way wondering, I renew

Some sense of common right;

And through my armour of imposition

Win the spring's keen light

Till for the woods against the world

I kiss the aconite